CORE WRITING SKILLS

How to
Write an Opinion Piece

Sara Howell

PowerKiDS
press.

New York

Published in 2014 by The Rosen Publishing Group, Inc.
29 East 21st Street, New York, NY 10010

First Edition

Editor: Amelie von Zumbusch
Book Design: Andrew Povolny
Photo Research: Katie Stryker

Photo Credits: Cover Mark Hall/The Image Bank/Getty Images; p. 4 DAJ/Getty Images; p. 5 John Howard/Lifesize/Thinkstock; p. 7 Altrendo Images/Stockbyte/Getty Images; p. 8 Vietrov Dmytro/Shutterstock.com; p. 9 Lorraine Swanson/Shutterstock.com; p. 10 Holly Kuchera/Shutterstock.com; p. 12 Flashon Studio/Shutterstock.com; p. 15 KidStock/Blend Images/Getty Images; p. 17 Martin Valigursky/Shutterstock.com; p. 18 Howard Sochurek/Time & Life Pictures/Getty Images; p. 21 Mark Bowden/The Agency Collection/Getty Images; p. 22 Nick White/Photodisc/Thinkstock.

Library of Congress Cataloging-in-Publication Data

Howell, Sara.
  How to write an opinion piece / Sara Howell. — First edition.
      pages cm. — (Core writing skills)
  Includes index.
  ISBN 978-1-4777-2906-9 (library binding) — ISBN 978-1-4777-2995-3 (pbk.) — ISBN 978-1-4777-3065-2 (6-pack)
  1. Authorship—Juvenile literature. 2. Book reviewing—Juvenile literature. 3. Persuasion (Rhetoric)—Juvenile literature. I. Title.
  PN159.H693 2014
  808.02—dc23
                            2013018987

Manufactured in the United States of America

CPSIA Compliance Information: Batch #W14PK4: For Further Information contact Rosen Publishing, New York, New York at 1-800-237-9932

CONTENTS

WHAT IS AN OPINION PIECE?

Like most people, you probably have some very strong opinions. An opinion is a belief based on what a person thinks. You might believe hamburgers taste better than hot dogs, cats make great pets, and your bedtime should be an hour later. Writing your beliefs down in an opinion piece is your chance to tell people what you think!

Writing an opinion piece is a good way to share your opinion on subjects about which you feel strongly. Reading an opinion piece you wrote aloud is as well.

If your opinion piece makes a good argument, with plenty of supporting facts, it might even change a reader's mind!

Writing Tip

A fact is something that can be proven true or false. You can use facts to explain why you hold an opinion.

In an opinion piece, you will **support**, or back up, your opinion with reasons or facts. Knowing how to express, or share, your opinion clearly is very important. Throughout history, well-written opinion pieces have changed peoples' minds about very important **issues**.

TOPICS AND TEXTS

There are two main types of opinion pieces. The first asks for your opinion on a certain **topic**, or issue. For example, do you think there should be a traffic light in front of your school? There are at least two sides to every issue. Decide which side you are on and then support your opinion.

Another type of opinion piece is called a **review**. Teachers often ask students to write reviews of books or other **texts**. A book review will list a book's good points and bad points. Reviews help other people decide whether or not they should read the book.

Writing Tip

A great way to start a book review is by asking yourself if you would recommend the book to a friend and why.

These kids are strongly opposed to the use of nuclear power. What topics do you feel strongly about?

PLANNING YOUR PIECE

Before you start writing your opinion piece, you will need to have an opinion! Find out as much as you can about your topic. Consider both sides of the issue, and then take a stand. If you are writing about the building of a new dog park, are you for the dog park or against it?

Have you ever had your opinion on a subject changed by something that you read?

If you are writing an opinion piece arguing that your school should have a hockey team, find out about hockey teams at other schools.

Writing Tip

Read newspapers and search the Internet for information on your topic. You can ask other people what their opinions are, too!

Your opinion piece will need a **structure**, or form, that will keep your ideas **organized** and clear. First, state your opinion. Then give reasons why you hold that opinion. End your piece with a strong **conclusion**, or ending.

THE INTRODUCTION

Your opinion piece should start with an **introduction**. This first section lets readers know what your topic is and where you stand. When you begin writing, it is important to know your **audience**, or the people reading your piece.

If you are writing an opinion piece about a plan to reintroduce wolves to your area, start your introduction by telling your audience about that plan.

> The BFG is a book about a friendly giant and a girl named Sophie. It was written by Roald Dahl and illustrated by Quentin Blake. I think it is a great, funny book.

Introduce the topic.

Give your audience background information.

State your opinion

Are you writing for your teacher, parents, or other students? The words and tone, or mood, of your piece should match the audience.

You should also consider whether your audience is familiar with the topic. That will help you decide how much time to spend explaining the issue. As you end the introduction, state your opinion.

Writing Tip

When writing for adults, keep your language formal. If you are writing for other kids, you can be more informal.

BE SPECIFIC!

The next section of your opinion piece will give the reasons why you hold your opinion. When listing your reasons, use **specific** examples whenever possible. You should also say where you found your information.

You might want to do some research to find facts to support your opinion. Books are a good source for facts. You can search for facts online, too.

Another reason we should have a longer recess is that it will make it easier to pay attention in class afterward. A study published by Yeshiva University researchers in 2009 found this.

Fact

Source

For example, if you are against putting a traffic light in front of your school, give specific reasons why. You might say that, according to the Wyoming Department of Transportation, traffic lights cause more rear-end collisions, or accidents. You might also suggest that the money for a traffic light would be better spent on hiring a crossing guard.

Writing Tip

It is a good idea to list at least three reasons why you hold an opinion. Each reason should get its own paragraph, or section.

ORGANIZING YOUR IDEAS

Sometimes you may have trouble explaining why you like or dislike a book or have a certain opinion about a topic. Creating a **graphic organizer** called a topic web is a great way to get your ideas on paper. Start by writing the name of the book or the issue in the middle of a piece of paper.

Topic Web About Hart's Ice Cream

Donate to local groups	Have been in town over 25 years

Great owners

In walking distance

Hart's Ice Cream Is My Favorite Store

Great flavors

More than 40 flavors

New flavors each week

Organizing your ideas and opinions can be hard. A graphic organizer can help, though.

Writing Tip

Writing down all the ideas that come into your head is called brainstorming. Do not worry about being right or wrong while you are brainstorming.

Then quickly write down all the words and ideas that come into your mind. Each new idea should branch out from the center.

You probably won't use all the ideas that you write down. Just get your imagination flowing!

LINKING WORDS

A link is a connection between two things. Linking words, such as "because," "since," and "therefore," show connections between your opinion and your reasons.

For example, your opinion may be that poodles are the best dogs. You may write that poodles are the best dogs because they have a special coat of fur. Since they have only one coat of fur, their hair does not shed very much. Therefore, poodles make great pets for people who have allergies to other dogs. The linking words here connect your ideas and show how your reasons support your opinion.

Writing Tip

Use linking words to connect two parts of a sentence. You can also use them to show the connections between sentences and paragraphs.

Can you find the linking word in the following sentence? Golden retrievers are my favorite dogs because they are very friendly.

IN CONCLUSION

Let's say you have stated your opinion and supported it with reasons in the body of your piece. Now it is time to write your conclusion. In a conclusion, you should summarize, or restate, the supporting facts that you listed to back up your opinion in a few sentences. Linking words can be especially helpful as you tie your ideas together.

If you are writing an opinion piece about who your hero is, you might want to end by quoting some inspiring words that that person said.

> We should reelect Katie Ryan class president. She was a good president this year, is nice to everyone, and is very organized. She'll do a great job next year, too!

Restate opinion.

Review supporting facts.

Include a new idea.

You should also state your opinion one more time. You can end with some famous words about your topic or a line from the book you are reviewing. Your conclusion should remind readers what you think and why. Be creative!

Writing Tip

A conclusion should add new information or state your reasons in a new way. Don't just repeat what you have already written.

SPREADING THE WORD

Today, many students use **technology**, such as computers and tablets, to help them do research and write. If you are using a computer, good keyboarding skills let you type quickly and make fewer mistakes. Programs that check your spelling are useful, too.

You can also use technology to share your piece. If your topic is important to your town or state, try emailing your piece to your mayor or state senator. With a parent's permission, you could even use your piece to start a **blog**. Technology can help you share your opinion with people all over the world!

Writing Tip

You can use the Internet to research your topic. Government websites and those connected to zoos, museums, and newspapers are great places to start.

Using a computer or tablet will also make it easier to revise, or make changes in, your opinion piece as you are working on it.

21

AN OPINION SANDWICH

Imagine the organizational structure of your opinion piece as a sandwich. The top piece of bread is your introduction. The meat, cheese, and lettuce are your supporting reasons. The bottom piece of bread is your conclusion. Like a sandwich, your opinion piece works best when it has the right structure.

Different people often hold very different opinions. Remember that, unlike facts, opinions are not right or wrong. An opinion piece is a chance to share your views and even change other people's opinions.

Have you ever had to write an opinion piece? What topic did you choose to write about?

GLOSSARY

audience (AH-dee-ints) A group of people who watch, listen to, or read something.

blog (BLOG) A place for people to report their thoughts or findings on the Internet.

conclusion (kun-KLOO-zhun) The last part or ending of something.

graphic organizer (GRA-fik OR-guh-ny-zer) A chart, graph, or picture that sorts facts and ideas and makes them clear.

introduction (in-truh-DUK-shun) A beginning part that explains what is going to follow.

issues (IH-shooz) Subjects with which people must deal.

organized (OR-guh-nyzd) Neat and in order.

review (rih-VYOO) A written opinion that lists something's good and bad points.

specific (spih-SIH-fik) Stated in a way that is clearly and easily understood.

structure (STRUK-cher) A way of making or organizing something.

support (suh-PORT) To give backing to someone or something.

technology (tek-NAH-luh-jee) Advanced tools that help people do and make things.

texts (TEKSTS) Pieces of writing.

topic (TAH-pik) The subject of a piece of writing.

INDEX

WEBSITES

Due to the changing nature of Internet links, PowerKids Press has developed an online list of websites related to the subject of this book. This site is updated regularly. Please use this link to access the list: www.powerkidslinks.com/cws/opin/

22·60